HAL•LEONARD VIOLIN PLAY-ALONG

VOL. 32

Favorite CHRISTMAS SONGS

Violin by Jon C. Wagoner

Audio Arrangements by Peter Deneff

Produced and Recorded by Jake Johnson at Paradyme Productions

ISBN 978-1-4768-1294-6

HAL•LEONARD® CORPORATION
7777 W. BLUEMOUND RD. P.O. BOX 13819 MILWAUKEE, WI 53213

Favorite CHRISTMAS SONGS

CONTENTS

Believe

from Warner Bros. Pictures' THE POLAR EXPRESS

Words and Music by Glen Ballard and Alan Silvestri

5

Have Yourself a Merry Little Christmas

from MEET ME IN ST. LOUIS

Words and Music by Hugh Martin and Ralph Blane

Let It Snow! Let It Snow! Let It Snow!

Words by Sammy Cahn
Music by Jule Styne

It's Beginning to Look Like Christmas

By Meredith Willson

Coda

Sleigh Ride

By Leroy Anderson

Somewhere in My Memory

from the Twentieth Century Fox Motion Picture HOME ALONE
Words by Leslie Bricusse
Music by John Williams

Winter Wonderland

Words by Dick Smith
Music by Felix Bernard

Walking in the Air

from THE SNOWMAN
Words and Music by Howard Blake